British Energy Policy and the
Threat to Manufacturing Industry

British Energy Policy and the Threat to Manufacturing Industry

Ruth Lea
and
Jeremy Nicholson

Civitas: Institute for the Study of Civil Society
London

First published July 2010

Previously published as a Civitas Online Report April 2010

© Civitas 2010
55 Tufton Street
London SW1P 3QL
Civitas is a registered charity (no. 1085494)
and a company limited by guarantee, registered in
England and Wales (no. 04023541)

email: books@civitas.org.uk

ISBN 978-1-906837-17-4

Independence: Civitas: Institute for the Study of Civil Society is a registered educational charity (No. 1085494) and a company limited by guarantee (No. 04023541). Civitas is financed from a variety of private sources to avoid over-reliance on any single or small group of donors.

Typeset by
Civitas

Printed in Great Britain by
Cromwell Press Group
Trowbridge, Wiltshire

Contents

Authors

Ruth Lea is currently Economic Adviser and Director of Arbuthnot Banking Group plc. Her previous jobs include the Director of the Centre for Policy Studies, Head of the Policy Unit at the Institute of Directors and Economics Editor at ITN. She also worked for six years in the City with Mitsubishi Bank and Lehmans and 16 years in the Civil Service including the Treasury and DTI.

Jeremy Nicholson is Director of the Energy Intensive Users Group, which campaigns for secure, competitive energy supplies for UK industry. He trained originally as a civil engineer and he spent four years as an economic analyst working for a group of French-owned water companies in the UK before joining EIUG, initially as their Economic Adviser, in 2000. He is a Board member of the International Federation of Industrial Consumers, a member of Ofgem's Environmental Advisory Group, the government's Business Energy Forum, and a Fellow of the Energy Institute.

Acknowledgement

We are very grateful to the ERA Foundation for a grant towards the cost of this publication.

1

British Energy Policy

Introduction

British energy policy has been inextricably tied up with climate change policy, which is principally concerned with cutting greenhouse gas emissions, especially CO_2, in order to 'tackle climate change'. Even though this paper will not discuss climate change policies in detail, it is relevant to note that they assume that:

- First, there will be damaging global warming over the next century, which should be mitigated.

- Secondly, such warming is principally driven by manmade, anthropogenic greenhouse gas emissions, principally carbon dioxide (CO_2). It is therefore necessary to cut these emissions in order to mitigate anthropogenic global warming (AGW).

- Thirdly, Britain's policies to dramatically cut carbon emissions will be supported by a truly global response. As Britain's share of manmade carbon emissions is less than two per cent of the global total, even if the British economy was completely 'decarbonised' it would have little impact on the total unless supported by the large emitters.[1]

Even if one has doubts about these assumptions, a focus on cutting back carbon emissions could be providing a useful catalyst for developing alternative technologies, for energy security reasons, enabling the British economy to reduce its exposure to the risks associated with growing dependence on imported fossil fuels. Unfortunately, the recent Labour Government's default position was to develop new gas-fired stations, which would be increasingly dependent on imported natural gas. The undoubted increased costs of energy arising from carbon reducing policies are already having serious implications for energy consumers—both business and domestic—which are set to intensify significantly.

The British Government has two major legislative commitments concerning CO_2 emissions reduction and the interlinked aim of dramatically increasing the proportion of energy, especially electricity, produced from renewable sources.

The first piece of legislation relates to the Climate Change Act (2008) which includes the following provisions:[2]

- A legally binding target of at least an 80 per cent cut in greenhouse gas (GHG) emissions by 2050, to be achieved through action in the UK and abroad. It also includes a reduction in emissions subsequently agreed to be at least 34 per cent by 2020. Both these targets are against a 1990 baseline. The EU's target for carbon cuts in 2020 compared with the 1990 baseline is much lower—'at least' 20 per cent.[3]

- A carbon budgeting system which caps emissions over five-year periods, with three budgets set at a time, to help emissions 'stay on track' for the 2050 target. The first three carbon budgets will run for the successive five year periods of 2008-2012, 2013-2017 and 2018-2022. In 2009, the Labour Government claimed that compared with the baseline, a cut of 21 per cent had already been achieved for 2008-2012.[4]

Two points need to be made concerning these targets. The first is that the 'easy' emission cuts have already been made and emissions cuts from now on will be far harder to achieve than in the past. The bulk of the falls in emissions since 1990 came from the switch away from coal-fired power stations and into gas, which emits less CO_2 per unit of output. The loss of heavy industry and manufacturing also contributed.

The second point is that even though the UK may be domestically emitting less carbon than in 1990, it is arguably actually responsible for increased global emissions over this period. If emissions caused by producing goods imported from overseas (many of which used to be produced here) are added in and aviation and shipping emissions 'costs' are taken into account, it has been calculated that UK carbon 'consumption' actually increased by 19 per cent between 1990 and 2005.[5]

The second piece of legislation is the EU's Renewables Directive (2008), under which the UK has a target of meeting 15 per cent of its final energy consumption through renewable sources by 2020.[6] The equivalent figure in 2005 was less than 1.5 per cent. One implication is that the share of electricity generated from renewable sources is officially projected to rise from the current 5.5 per cent to around 30 per cent by 2020. Few commentators believe that this target is achievable.[7] The Renewables Directive is discussed further below.

Energy and climate change policies: increased costs

The recent Labour Government's climate change strategy proved to be costly for both domestic and business energy consumers as its policies significantly raised electricity costs. There are three ways in which costs have been imposed:[8]

- The Renewables Obligation (RO): The RO is the obligation placed on licensed electricity suppliers to deliver a specified amount of their electricity from eligible renewable sources. It was introduced in 2002 to incentivise the generation of electricity from eligible renewable sources in the UK. The costs associated with the RO are rising as the obligation levels are rising.

- The EU's Emissions Trading System (ETS): The ETS is an EU-wide 'cap and trade' scheme which started in 2005. Phase I ran from 2005 to 2007, phase II is currently operative (2008 to 2012). The allocation of free permits is due to be substantially reduced under phase III (2013-2020), which will increase the price of electricity generated from fossil fuels.

- The Climate Change Levy (CCL): The CCL is a tax on the use of energy in industry, commerce and the public sector (i.e. all non-domestic sectors) intended to reduce energy use and hence CO_2 emissions. It was introduced in April 2001. There are exemptions but, notably, nuclear-generated electricity is not one of them—despite the fact such generation has no CO_2 emissions.

According to official estimates released by BERR in June 2008 at the launch of the Labour Government's lengthy consultation into the *Renewable Energy Strategy*, climate change policies had already added 21 per cent to the average business electricity bill and 14 per cent to domestic bills.[9,10] At that time BERR estimated that these policies would add 55 per cent (34 per cent higher than in 2008) to the average business electricity bill by 2020 and 18 per cent to domestic bills. The Labour Government's climate change policies also added to gas bills: four per cent to business bills and three per cent to domestic bills.

DECC's latest cost estimates

On 15 July 2009, following the renewables consultation and the enactment of the Climate Change Act, Britain's Labour Government released a series of documents updating their estimates of the costs of meeting both the renewables and the carbon reduction targets.

The main document was DECC's *The Renewable Energy Strategy*, which mapped how the UK's 15 per cent renewables target by 2020 would be achieved.[11, 12] Costs for a new package of measures covering energy efficiency policies as well as those intended to meet the renewables target (in addition to those already in place) were included. The lead scenario in this paper suggested that by 2020:

- More than 30 per cent of electricity generated would be from renewables, mostly in the form of onshore and offshore wind, up from about 5.5 per cent today.

- 12 per cent of heat would be generated from renewables, up from very low levels today.

- 10 per cent of transport energy would come from renewables, up from the current level of 2.6 per cent of road transport consumption.

The estimated costs of the *additional* measures necessary to achieve these 'targets' for electricity and gas bills are shown in the tables below. And, as the Strategy paper (paragraph 7.32) stated:

- '…we estimate that, if taken in isolation, the measures included in this Strategy would increase … [non-domestic energy bills] by an average 15 per cent for electricity and 30 per cent for gas by 2020'.

It is likely that these costs would be 'over and above' those quoted in the consultation document (June 2008), though there could be some degree of overlap between the renewable element of the 55 per cent cost increase (i.e. the RO as currently constituted) and the additional measures required to meet the renewable target.

Table 1.1: Effects on annual domestic and non-domestic electricity bills resulting from additional measures to achieve about 30 per cent renewable electricity

	Domestic		Non-domestic
	Average bill impact	% impact	% impact
2015	£12	2%	2%
2020	£77	15%	15%

Source: HM Government, *The UK Renewable Energy Strategy*, July 2009, tables 7.2 and 7.4, central case, oil price assumption: $80pb.

Table 1.2: Effects on annual domestic and non-domestic gas bills resulting from additional measures to achieve about 12% renewable heat

	Domestic		Non-domestic
	Average bill impact	% impact	% impact
2015	£34	5%	6%
2020	£172	23%	30%

Source: HM Government, *The UK Renewable Energy Strategy*, July 2009, tables 7.3 and 7.5, central case, oil price assumption: $80pb.

Table 1.3: Total cost effects on business and domestic bills resulting from all renewables / climate change measures for electricity

	Business	Domestic
Current policies (June 2008 estimates) for 2008	+21%	+14%
Current policies (June 2008 estimates) for 2020	+55%	+18%
Additional measures (July 2009) for 2020	+15%	+15%
Maximum total for 2020	+70%	+33%

Sources: (i) June 2008 data: BERR, *UK Renewable Energy Strategy consultation document*, June 2008. (ii) July 2009 data: HM Government, *The UK Renewable Energy Strategy*, July 2009.

On this basis, business would be facing additional costs on electricity bills of up to 70 per cent, depending on the degree of overlap already referred to, because of 'green' policies by 2020. Even the domestic sector could face 'green' costs of up to 33 per cent on their bills. Continuing on the theme of the costs of these renewables/climate change policies, the impact assessments of the *Renewable Energy Strategy* were released alongside the main document in July 2009. They predicted that the net costs of the strategy for the period 2010-2030 could range between £52bn and £66bn (in 2008 prices).[12] By no stretch of the imagination can these extra costs imposed on the economy be regarded as nugatory.

The other documents were:[13]

- DECC, *The UK Low Carbon Transition Plan*, which outlined the path as to how the 34 per cent carbon emission cuts by 2020, compared with 1990, would be achieved.

- BIS and DECC, *The UK Low Carbon Industrial Strategy (LCIS)*, which set out a series of active government interventions to support industries critical to 'tackling climate change'.[14]

- DfT, *The Low Carbon Transport Plan*, which set out how to reduce carbon emissions from domestic transport by up to14 per cent over the next decade.

Chart 1.1: Growth required in renewable energy production to meet EU Renewables Targets (as % total energy, 2005 – 2010)

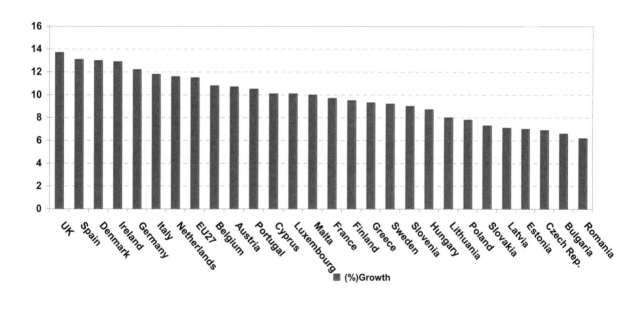

Source: European Commission and see annex 2, table 1 for the detailed figures

The EU Renewables Directive: the UK's challenge

A key issue for Britain's energy cost competitiveness, as will be discussed further in chapter 2, is whether the UK's low carbon policies will push up energy prices more for UK producers than the equivalent policies in other countries. Considering the EU Renewables

Directive alone, it is clear that the UK will be at a considerable cost disadvantage compared with other EU members.

Chart 1.1 above shows the growth in renewables required to hit the national targets for renewables' share in final energy consumption in 2020. As can be seen from this table, the UK faces the greatest challenge in reaching its 2020 target, followed by Spain and Denmark. The UK's position is made all the harder by starting with a very modest renewables industry—the proportion of renewables to total energy consumption in 2005 was just 1.3 per cent, compared with an EU27 average of 8.5 per cent. By contrast several EU countries are relatively well-placed including most of the central and eastern EU countries and Sweden, Greece, Finland and France.

The EU Renewables Directive: costs for the UK

Leaving aside whether the UK target is achievable, and doubts have already been expressed in this paper, it is vital to consider the potential relative costs of achieving the target. A study conducted by Pöyry Energy Consulting for BERR in March 2008 clearly showed that the UK would bear the greatest cost burden of the Directive.[15] Pöyry developed two scenarios for the EU as a whole:

- The central case least-cost trading scenario. This assumed that a market for trading renewable certificates would develop, enabling the most efficient deployment of renewable resources to be achieved throughout the EU.

- A domestic-constrained scenario. This assumed that no market for trading permits would develop and, therefore, Member States would have to meet their targets solely through domestic resources.

Pöyry's main cost estimates, discounted back to 2006, are shown in the table below for these two scenarios.[16]

Table 1.4: Compliance costs of meeting the 2020 renewables target, €bn

	EU total	UK total	UK % of EU total
Annual cost (in 2020):			
Least cost	18.8	5.0	26.6%
Domestic-constrained	25.6	6.7	26.2%
Lifetime costs (up to 2020):			
Least cost	259.0	59.0	22.8%
Domestic-constrained	351.7	93.1	26.5%

Source: Pöyry Energy Consulting Report, table 4.

The UK's share of the EU costs of complying with the Directive was, therefore, estimated to be around a quarter of total EU costs, greater than for any other major EU member state. The relatively high costs were due to a combination of the huge investment required to hit the target and the UK's favoured choice of investment in expensive, intermittent wind power. The potential effects of this Directive alone clearly disadvantage the UK.

The UK's extra tight carbon cuts targets by 2020, 34 per cent under the Climate Change Act compared with the EU's 20 per cent, are likely to add further to the deterioration in the UK's energy competitiveness vis-à-vis other EU states. This analysis excludes consideration of countries outside the EU, of course. Few of these countries appear to be adopting tough low carbon policies and the deterioration in Britain's energy competitiveness against these economies will be even more acute than against EU countries.

Chart 1.2: Industrial electricity prices, extra large users, pence/kWh (inc. taxes), selected EU countries, to the first half of 2009.

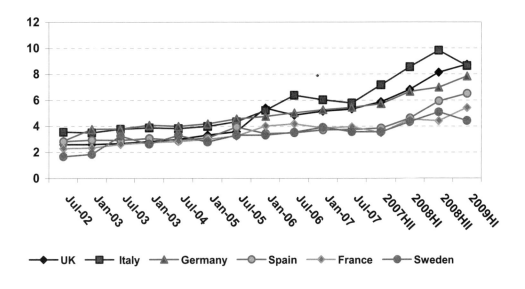

Source: DECC, Quarterly energy prices, December 2009, Eurostat data

Energy costs: EU comparisons

Finally, it is worth noting that, even without the extra costs associated with climate change policies that are due to be imposed in forthcoming years, Britain has already tended to have relatively expensive energy costs. The chart below shows the electricity prices for extra large users in selected EU countries. With the exception of Italy, which has inadequate generating capacity, UK industrial electricity prices have consistently exceeded those of the other major economies. In recent years, industrial prices have been almost double those in nuclear/hydro-dependent France and Sweden. In the first half of 2009 British prices even exceeded those of Italy.

It should be pointed out that, during the beginning of 2010, the UK's relative energy prices position improved because of the global gas glut and relatively high UK electricity supply margins. But as the world economy recovers these temporary advantages are not expected to persist and prices are therefore expected to rise.[17] And these increases can be expected to occur irrespective of the additional impact of unilateral climate change policies on supply costs.

2

The Impact of High Energy Costs
on Energy Intensive Users

Introduction

As the economy struggles to emerge from the economic crisis of 2008-2009, the manufacturing sector will contribute positively to the general recovery and the rebalancing of the economy. Under these circumstances it is politic to ensure that manufacturing industries are supported by government policies that help rather than hinder their competitiveness. This is not a case of special pleading for subsidies for manufacturing industries, but rather this is about maintaining a competitive level playing field for British industry.

These policies areas include competitive tax and regulatory regimes, good infrastructure and competitive transport costs, a skilled and motivated labour force and competitive and reliable energy supplies.[1] One of the main conclusions of a roundtable discussion for senior industrialists in 2009 was that one of the top issues that should be tackled urgently is energy costs—along with improving technical skills.[2]

But, as we explained in chapter 1, British energy costs could increase significantly in forthcoming years as a direct result of policies aimed at reducing carbon emissions and increasing the use of renewable energy, which will undermine the competitiveness of British businesses—especially energy intensive users. As also discussed in chapter 1, some of the carbon reduction policies originate in the EU and they will serve to undermine the competitiveness of the whole bloc. But Britain is in an especially disadvantageous position. There are two main reasons for this. Firstly, in addition to EU targets, the recent Labour Government adopted the tighter carbon reduction targets written into the Climate Change Act and, secondly, Britain's chosen route to meeting its highly ambitious EU renewables target depends on a huge expansion of expensive and intermittent wind power, which requires considerable conventional (i.e. fossil fuelled) back-up capacity.[3] In the rush to appear 'green', the British authorities seem to have neglected the significant competitiveness implications for many other businesses of their policy decisions.

Higher electricity prices: the 'green mark-up'

We also discussed in chapter 1 the recent Labour Government's estimates for the 'green mark-up' for industrial electricity prices. This mark-up reflects rising renewable obligation levels and the changes to the EU's Emissions Trading System (ETS), and could rise from 21 per cent (2008) to 'up to 70 per cent' in 2020. The allocation of free permits under the ETS is due to be substantially reduced under phase III (2013-2020), when the EU will start selling permits by auction. The free issue of permits for electricity generation will cease entirely. The cost of these permits will be boosted by the ETS's tough and declining 'cap' for carbon emissions.

Such extra costs would inevitably tilt the balance for energy intensive businesses and risk rendering them unviable in Britain. They will probably migrate to countries outside the ETS. In particular they will go to countries that have not made a big commitment to reduce CO_2 emissions such as China. In Brussels this competitive threat is known as 'carbon leakage'. Ironically, this could well lead to net global increases in carbon emissions associated with British product demand because Chinese emissions per unit of output are likely to exceed the equivalent emissions from the British plants they could displace, given the greater prevalence of coal-based technology in China. In addition, there are the CO_2 emissions associated with shipping the displaced products.

This is surely *not* what the ETS aimed to achieve. The ETS aimed to cut global carbon emissions. But it could increase them. And in the absence of mitigating measures for vulnerable industries, it could wreck significant parts of British industrial base in the process. Doubts have already been expressed about the future of some of Britain's oil refining plants, given the higher energy costs.[4]

At the Copenhagen Summit on climate change in December 2009 the EU was effectively ignored and isolated.[5] Given the ETS's threats to EU industries in general and Britain's in particular, the EU should surely reconsider aspects of its energy and climate change policies.

Energy intensive industries

Energy intensive industries can broadly be defined as those which necessarily have high energy consumption in their production processes and, therefore, energy costs tend to comprise a large proportion of their overall cost base. They include the following industries: steel, glass and ceramics, bulk chemicals, industrial gases, paper, aluminium and cement production.

The proportion of total costs attributable to energy inputs clearly depends on how relatively expensive energy is to other inputs. But the EIUG estimates that energy related production costs as a percentage of total costs currently amount to around 20-25 per cent for the steel, paper, glass and cement industries, 40 per cent for aluminium smelting and as high as 70 per cent for industrial gases.

Britain is already losing energy intensive businesses because of the lack of competitiveness—this is discussed below. But, given the expected increasing international cost differentials, Britain looks set to lose more to lower cost locations. In global markets many British energy intensive businesses will not be able to compete—not because they are inefficient, they are not, but because their overall cost base is simply too high.

The direct contribution of energy intensive industries to GDP is around one per cent according to the EIUG. But this is the tip of the iceberg of their significance in the overall economy because they facilitate and support dependent British 'downstream' industries which would probably also close if they closed.

An example of the relationship between the energy intensive using industry and its inter-dependent 'downstream' industries is furnished by the chemicals industry where chlor-alkali production supports 'downstream' industries ranging from PVC, soaps and detergents to sewage treatment. If chlor-alkali production were to stop in Britain, much of the rest of the chemicals industry could disappear too. The chemicals industry will be further discussed below.

The primary chemicals industry and the other energy intensive industries are sometimes dismissed as 'sunset' industries as if they had no place in Britain's modern 'post-industrial age' economy. This betrays a failure to realise how 'state of the art' and high-tech these businesses are, the steel industry being a notable example, and it highlights a failure to understand their role in the interdependent modern economy where they are at the hub of modern and technically sophisticated spin-off industries. It also betrays an extraordinary indifference to industries which, in their own right, contribute to GDP and the balance of payments and are important employers—crucially—across the regions of the UK.

The impact of high energy prices

There is no doubt that high energy prices have already been a factor behind industry closures. In 2003 the energy intensive Britannia Zinc works near Bristol was closed, with a loss of 400 jobs.[6] And in May 2006 the EIUG reported that the UK gas price spike of 2005-06 had contributed to 6,000 jobs lost over the previous 18 months in the glass sector; several paper mills had also been closed.[7] In addition, brick capacity had been cut back and manufacturers of chlorine and ammonia-based fertilizer had reduced production. In July 2006 EIUG reported that even where production was continuing investment was being reduced, thus cutting back the potential capacity and potential contribution of these businesses to employment and GDP.[8]

Anglesey Aluminium's plant closed last year, following the ending of its deal to buy competitively priced electricity from the nearby Wylfa nuclear power station, which had recently passed into state ownership.[9] Under EU law the electricity deal with the now state-owned Wylfa was classified as 'state aid' and therefore deemed illegal. Of Britain's two other primary aluminium plants, the one at Lynemouth in Northumberland uses electricity from its own coal-fired power station.[10] This power station will require the fitting of costly scrubbers in order to comply technically with the EU's Large Combustion Plants Directive even though they will have no improved environmental impact because the air quality is already controlled using another, more sophisticated, procedure. Such extra costs will inevitably undermine the economic viability of the plant.

It is important to note that high energy prices are not just damaging energy intensive industrial businesses. It was reported last year that high electricity prices, then quoted as the third highest in Europe, were a factor in forcing companies to locate power-hungry data centres outside Britain.[11] Uncompetitive energy prices are therefore undermining the British economy across a wide spectrum of businesses. Suffice to say at this point, the regressive impact of high energy prices on less well-off households is outside the remit of this paper.

Chemicals industry—a case study: INEOS Chlor

The chemicals industry, including pharmaceuticals, has been one Britain's most successful manufacturing sectors. Its growth since 1970 is shown in the chart below.[12] Engineering, including aerospace equipment, has also grown well. Metals, including steel, and, especially, textiles are the clear losers since 1970.

The chemicals industry currently represents around 11-12 per cent of the value of UK manufacturing output and the chemical sector provides direct employment for 214,000 people and supports 'several 100,000' additional jobs throughout the economy.[13] Large chemicals works are located in the regions outside the prosperous South-East: including Grangemouth, Runcorn (Cheshire), Teesside and the Humber Estuary. Importantly, there is expertise across the chemicals spectrum: commodity chemicals, specialty chemicals and consumer chemicals.

Chart 2.1: Selected sub-sectors of manufacturing industry, volume data, 2003=100, 1970-2008

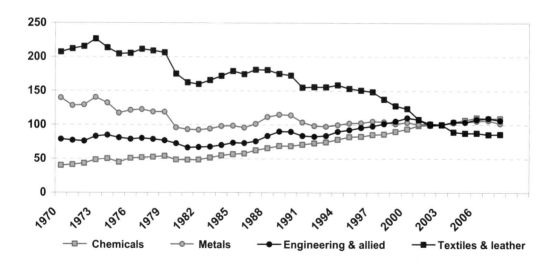

Source: ONS database. The chart omits: coke & allied industries; food, drink & tobacco; and 'other' manufactures (including paper & printing, rubber & plastics, and other non-metallic mineral products).

The chemicals industry, by the very nature of its business, is about integrating processes and finding small margins in a business that has huge fixed costs in plant, equipment and energy.

One such plant is the INEOS Chlor plant at Runcorn which has the second largest 'cell room', where chlorine is extracted from brine, in Europe. Caustic soda is also produced in the process. The plant is a heavy user of electricity. There are no viable low energy consuming manufacturing alternatives available to the business—the process is limited by the laws of thermodynamics. The economic viability of the plant is, therefore, heavily dependent on the cost of electricity.

Under phase III of the EU's ETS the INEOS Chlor plant should get a free allocation of permits covering most of its direct carbon emissions, but, crucially, most of its emissions will be indirect through its electricity inputs and, as we have already discussed, the prices of these electricity inputs are set to rise very significantly indeed. The hike in electricity prices will mean that INEOS Chlor, in the judgement of management, will quite simply be uncompetitive with its foreign competitors—especially outside the EU. Under these circumstances it will go out of business unless there is government support. While the ETS Directive does make provision for the payment of compensation, it is not clear whether this will be forthcoming from the UK's new coalition government.

The INEOS Chlor plant is a significant business in its own right. But its overall economic significance is far greater because the chlorine and caustic soda produced at Runcorn are used throughout the UK in extensive and wide-ranging 'downstream' industries:

- Chlorine, a commodity chemical, is vital to the modern and diverse chemicals industry and has a huge variety of uses. It is used as a disinfectant and purifier, and in the manufacture of plastics (Polyvinyl chloride, PVC), solvents, agrochemicals and pharmaceuticals. It is also an intermediate in manufacturing other substances where it is not contained in the final product. Products reliant on chlorine's unique properties include household items such as bleach and disinfectant to bullet-resistant vests, computer hardware, silicon chips and automotive parts.

- Caustic soda is used for making many products including soaps and detergents.

If the Runcorn plant were to close, then the chances are that many of the 'downstream' industries would close too. Rather than import the basic chemicals, many of the downstream businesses would migrate to countries where they were still domestically produced for reasons of reliability of supply and transport costs. The long-term continuation of chlor-alkali production in Britain is vitally important for these businesses.

INEOS Chlor commissioned a study of the possible 'fall out' if the Runcorn chlor-alkali plant were to close.[14] The main conclusions were:

- The numbers of direct jobs within the UK chemical industry threatened within a period of approximately 10 years was estimated to be about 46,000. Industry revenue losses estimated to reach about £8bn per year over that period.

- There would be a further 87,000 jobs threatened in the wider economy.

- And the *total* number of jobs likely to be lost in the long-term, throughout the industry, its suppliers and consumer goods and services industries is in the region of 133,000, with revenue losses of some £17bn.

- The losses were mainly in the English regions of the North-West, North-East and the West Midlands and in Scotland.

- All in all, the closure of chlor-alkali capacity in Runcorn would result in significant damage to the downstream chemical industries, with inevitable knock-on effects into the wider economy.

- It was estimated that the loss of annual revenues to the UK government were estimated to be about £1.6bn.

The composition of the job losses and the layers of 'fall out' from the Runcorn closure are shown in the table below.

Table 2.1: Stages of impact of Runcorn closure: the 'fall out' chart

	Businesses	Location	Directly dependent jobs lost	Jobs lost, in wider economy	Total jobs lost
Core impact	INEOS Chlor	Runcorn, Widnes, Warrington	3,000	6,000	9,000
Immediate impact – destroyed downstream industries	PVC, soaps & detergents, sewage treatment	Mersey-Manchester, Teesside, West Midlands	7,000	13,000	20,000
Intermediate – damaged related industries	Pharmaceuticals, food processing, toiletries	NW, NE, Yorkshire & Humberside, Scotland, other UK	23,000	43,000	66,000
Long term – disadvantaged industries	Consumer goods and services	All UK	13,000	25,000	38,000
TOTAL			46,000	87,000	133,000

Source: LECG Limited, Report to Ineos Chlor Limited, the evaluation of options for the chlor-alkali plant at Runcorn, main report, September 2001, adapted.

Annex 1: Glossary of Terms

Alternative energy: Alternative energy is a term used for some energy source that is an alternative to using fossil fuels. Generally, it indicates energies that are non-traditional (non conventional) and have low environmental impact. The term *alternative* is used to contrast with fossil fuels according to some sources, and some sources may use it interchangeably with renewable energy.

Biofuels: These comprise liquid or gaseous fuel for transport produced from biomass. They include: (i) biodiesel: produced from vegetable oils or animal fats by mixing them with ethanol or methanol to break the down and (ii) bioethanol: created from crops rich in starch or sugar by fermentation, distillation and finally dehydration.

Biomass: Products derived from plant or animal matter and includes agricultural, forestry wastes/residues and energy crops. It can be used for fuel directly by burning or extraction of combustible oils.

Business as usual (BAU): A term used in scenario building to denote broadly unchanged policy.

Capacity credit: The capacity credit of wind power expresses how much 'conventional' power can be avoided or replaced by wind power.

Carbon budgets: These budgets, introduced in the Climate Change Act (2008), set limits on the total greenhouse gas emissions (GHG) allowed from the UK in successive five year periods. The carbon budgets are part of DECC's 'Low Carbon Transition Plan' to a low carbon future. The first three budgets were announced in April 2009 and are (source: The Department of Energy and Climate Change):

- Budget 1, 2008-2012: 21 per cent reduction on 1990 levels—already achieved. 3018 million tonnes (Mt) CO_2e (CO_2 equivalent) emitted in this five-year period.

- Budget 2, 2013-2017: 2782 Mt CO_2e of emissions projected for this five-year period.

- Budget 3, 2018-2022: 2544 Mt CO_2e of emissions projected for this five-year period, 34 per cent reduction compared with 1990 level.

Clean Development Mechanism (CDM): This is an arrangement under the Kyoto Protocol (agreed in 1997 to cut greenhouse gas emissions) allowing industrialised countries with a greenhouse gas reduction commitment to invest in ventures that reduce emissions in developing countries as an alternative to more expensive emission reductions in their own countries. A crucial feature of an approved CDM carbon project is that it has established that the planned reductions would not occur without the additional incentive provided by emission reductions credits, a concept known as 'additionality'.

Climate change levy (CCL): The Climate change levy (CCL) is a tax on the use of energy in industry, commerce and the public sector (all non-domestic sectors) intended to encourage energy efficiency. It was introduced in April 2001 and is not carbon based. The CCL does not apply to the following (source: The Department of Energy and Climate Change):

- Oils, which are already subject to excise duty.

- Electricity generated from new renewable energy (such as solar and wind power) – but note that it applies to electricity generated by nuclear power stations.

- Fuel used by 'good quality combined heat and power' (CHP) schemes.

- Fuel used as a feedstock.

- Electricity used in electrolysis processes, such as the chlor-alkali process, or primary aluminium smelting.

Climate Change Act (2008): The Climate Change Bill, released in March 2007, became law on 26 November 2008.

The Climate Change Act creates a new approach to managing and responding to climate change in the UK, by:

- Setting ambitious, legally binding targets.

- Taking powers to help meet those targets.

- Strengthening the institutional framework.

- Enhancing the UK's ability to adapt to the impact of climate change.

- Establishing clear and regular accountability to the UK Parliament and to the devolved legislatures.

There are 2 key aims of the Act:

- To improve carbon management, helping the transition towards a low-carbon economy in the UK

- To demonstrate UK leadership internationally, signalling that the UK 'is committed to taking its share of responsibility for reducing global emissions in the context of developing negotiations on a post-2012 global agreement at Copenhagen in December 2009'.

Key provisions of the Act include:

- A legally binding target of at least an 80% cut in greenhouse gas (GHG) emissions by 2050, to be achieved through action in the UK and abroad. It also includes a reduction in emissions subsequently agreed to be at least 34% by 2020. Both these targets are against a 1990 baseline. This is tougher than the EU's '20:20:20 plan' (see EU Renewable Energy Directive (2008) below).

- A carbon budgeting system which caps emissions over five-year periods, with three 'carbon budgets' set at a time, to help the UK 'stay on track for the 2050 target'. The first three carbon budgets will run from 2008-12, 2013-17 and 2018-22. See note on carbon budgets above. *Source: The Department of Energy and Climate Change*

Combined Heat and Power (CHP): CHP is the simultaneous generation of usable heat and power (usually electricity) in a single process.

Conventional (traditional) energy sources: These are non-renewable energy (RE) sources.

Department of Business, Enterprise and Regulatory Reform (BERR): BERR was established in June 2007 mainly from most of the former Department of Trade and Industry (DTI) and the Better Regulation Executive (BRE). It was subsumed into BIS (see below) in June 2009.

Department of Business, Innovation and Skills (BIS): BERR was replaced by the Department of Business, Innovation and Skills (BIS), which incorporated the Department of Innovation, Universities and Skills in June 2009. *Website:* www.bis.gov.uk.

Department of Energy and Climate Change (DECC): The energy division of BERR and the climate change responsibilities of DEFRA were transferred to the new Department of Energy and Climate Change (DECC) in October 2008. *Website:* www.decc.gov.uk

Energy Intensive Users Group (EIUG): The EIUG's membership comprises trade associations and customer groups representing industrial sectors with the heaviest energy consumption in the UK. The sectors covered include steel, chemicals, paper, cement, glass, ceramics, aluminium and industrial gases.

EU Emissions Trading Scheme (EU ETS): see 'EU Emissions Trading System'.

EU Emissions Trading System (EU ETS): 2005-2012
Formerly referred to as the EU Emissions Trading *Scheme*, the EU Emissions Trading System (EU ETS) is one of the key policies introduced by the European Union originally to help meet its greenhouse gas emissions (GHG) target of eight per cent below 1990 levels under the Kyoto Protocol (for the years 2008-2012). It has the following features (source: The Department of Energy and Climate Change):

- The ETS is an EU-wide 'cap and trade' scheme and it started in 2005. Each Member State develops National Allocation Plans (NAPs), which are approved by the European Commission. This sets an overall cap on the total emissions allowed from all the installations covered by the System. This is converted into allowances (one allowance equals one tonne of CO_2) which are then distributed by EU member states to installations covered by the System. At the end of each year, installations are required to surrender allowances to account for their actual emissions. They may use all or part of their allocation. Installations can emit more than their allocation by buying allowances from the market. Similarly, an installation that emits less than its allocation can sell its surplus allowances. The environmental outcome is not affected because the amount of allowances allocated is fixed.

- The EU ETS covers electricity generation and the main energy-intensive industries – power stations, refineries and offshore, iron and steel, cement and lime, paper, food and drink, glass, ceramics, engineering and the manufacture of vehicles.

- The ETS (2005-2012) comprises phase I (2005-2007) and phase II (2008-2012).

EU Emissions Trading System (EU ETS): 2013-2020

The revised EU ETS Directive, signed in December 2008, is a central part of the EU Climate and Energy 2020 Package and will apply to phase III (2013-2020). The changes compared with phases I and II include (source: The Department of Energy and Climate Change):

- National Allocation Plans (NAPs) will become National Implementation Measures (NIMs) and from 2013 onwards most elements of the scheme will be determined at EU level.

- There will be no free allocation for electricity production in the UK and most other Member States. Permits will be auctioned, though free permits will be allocated to selected companies.

- Aviation will be included.

EU Renewable Energy Directive: 2001

The EU Directive on the 'Promotion of Electricity from Renewable Energy Sources in the Internal Electricity Market' (2001/77/EC), also known as the 'Renewables Directive', included:

- Member states were required to adopt national targets for renewables that are consistent with reaching the Commission's target of 22 per cent of electricity from renewables by 2010.

- The indicative target that the proposal sets for the UK was 10 per cent of electricity by that date.

- The directive also required that Member States ensure that a 'guarantee of origin' (GoO) was issued on request in respect of electricity generated from eligible renewable energy sources, as defined by the directive.

EU Renewable Energy Directive: 2008

Following on from commitments made in March 2007, this Directive was agreed in December 2008. Proposals include:

- Plans for a 20 per cent renewables contribution to total energy demand and a 20 per cent cut in greenhouse gas emissions (GHG) by 2020, the so-called '20:20:20 plan'.

- The deal, between the European Parliament, the French Presidency, on behalf of the Council, and the European Commission, means that more than one third of EU electricity must come from renewables by 2020.

- The Directive establishes national overall targets for each member state. These targets are shown in annex 2, table 1 below; the UK has agreed to a binding target of 15 per cent. A path of compliance is also set with interim targets every two years.

- The share of energy from renewable sources in transport in 2020 is at least 10 per cent of final energy consumption in transport.

- Trading of Guarantees of Origin (GoO) is allowed between member states, the trading partners will be the EU27 governments. A country is only allowed to trade its GoOs additional to its interim target, without obligation.

Fossil fuels: Coal, natural gas and fuels derived from crude oil (for example petrol and diesel) are called fossil fuels because they have been formed over long periods of time from ancient organic matter.

Fuel cells: These produce electricity from hydrogen and air, with water as the only emission. Potential applications include stationary power generation, transport (replacing the internal combustion engine (ICE)) and portable power (replacing batteries in mobile phones)

Fuel poverty: The common definition of a fuel poor household is one needing to spend in excess of 10 per cent of household income to achieve a satisfactory heating regime: 21 degrees centigrade in the living room and 18 degrees centigrade for other occupied rooms.

Guarantee of origin (GoO): This is a document which has the function of providing proof that a given quantity of energy was produced from renewable sources, introduced under the 2001 EU Renewables Directive. They are known as Renewable Energy Guarantees of Origin (REGOs) in GB. Under the 2008 Directive on renewables, trading of Guarantees of

Origin (GoO) will be allowed between member states and the trading partners will be the EU27 governments.

Kyoto protocol and the EU: The EU15 signed up to the Kyoto Protocol on the UN Framework Convention on Climate Change (UNFCCC) in 1997. The protocol agreed to cut Greenhouse Gas (GHG) emissions, of which CO_2 emissions are one of the most significant, by eight per cent by the five-year commitment period 2008-2012 (taking annual average emissions over this period) compared with the base year 1990.

Load factor: The actual amount of, say, kilowatt hours (KWh) delivered on a system in a designated period of time as opposed to the total possible kilowatt hours that could be delivered on a system in a designated period of time.

Low Carbon Transition Plan: This plan plots how the UK will meet the 34 per cent cut in emissions on 1990 levels by 2020, including carbon budgets and other policies in order to achieve this target. Three papers on low carbon policies were published in July 2009 along with the Renewable Energy Strategy.

Microgeneration: The generation of zero or low-carbon heat and power by individuals, small businesses and communities to meet their own needs. The Labour Government published the Microgeneration Strategy in March 2006. The aim was to create conditions under which microgenerators become a realistic alternative or supplementary energy source.

Non-energy use (of energy sources): This includes fuel used for chemical feedstock, solvents, lubricants and road making material.

Non-Fossil Fuel Obligation (NFFO): Before the introduction of the Renewables Obligation (RO), the NFFO was the Labour Government's major instrument for encouraging growth within the renewable energy industry. The NFFO applied in England and Wales. In Scotland and Northern Ireland, the Renewables Obligation (Scotland) (ROS) or the Northern Ireland NFFO (NI-NFFO) applied. The NFFO assisted the industry by providing premium payments for renewables-generated electricity over a fixed period, with contracts being awarded to individual generators.

Photovoltaics (PV): This refers to the direct conversion of solar radiation into electricity by the interaction of light with the electrons in a semiconductor device or cell.

Plant capacity: The maximum power available from a power station at a point in time.

Plant load factor: The plant load factor is the average hourly quantity of electricity supplied during the year, expressed as a percentage of the average output capability at the beginning and the end of the year. It is a measure of how intensively power stations are being used.

Primary fuels: fuels obtained directly from natural sources of energy. For example, coal, oil and natural gas.

Renewable energy (RE): This refers to energy flows that occur naturally and continuously in the environment, such as energy from the wind, waves or tides. The origin of the majority of these sources can be traced back to either the sun (energy from the sun helps to drive the earth's weather patterns) or the gravitational effects of the sun and the moon. This means that these sources are essentially inexhaustible but not 'free'—a popular misconception.

Renewable energy sources: These include solar power, wind, wave and tide, and hydroelectricity. Solid renewable energy sources consist of wood, straw, short rotation coppice, other biomass and biodegradable fraction of wastes. Gaseous renewables include landfill gas and sewage gas. Non-biodegradable wastes are not counted as a renewables source. There are three main uses: the generation of electricity, the provision of heat (thermal use) and transport.

Renewable Energy Guarantee of Origin (REGO): See also Guarantee of origin (GoO). The Electricity (Guarantees of Origin of Electricity Produced from Renewable Energy Sources) Regulations 2003 set out the requirements for the issue, transfer and revocation of REGOs in Great Britain. Under the regulations, Ofgem is responsible for issuing GB REGOs.

Renewable energy obligation: This is a national support scheme requiring energy producers to include a given proportion of energy from renewable sources in their production, requiring energy suppliers to include a given proportion of energy from renewable sources in their supply or requiring energy consumers to include a given proportion of energy from renewable sources in their consumption.

Renewable Energy Strategy: BERR launched the consultation on 'UK renewable energy strategy' in June 2008, concerned with the UK's 15% binding target by 2020 under the EU Renewables Directive (2008). In July 2009 DECC released a major paper, 'The Renewable Energy Strategy', in response. The lead scenario in this paper suggested that by 2020:

- 'More than 30 per cent of electricity generated will be from renewables, up from about 5.5 per cent today'.
- '12 per cent of heat will be generated from renewables, up from very low levels today'.

- And '10 per cent of transport energy will come from renewables, up from the current level of 2.6 per cent of road transport consumption'.

The Impact Assessments of the UK Renewable Energy Strategy are shown in annex 2, table 2 below. Other papers relating to a 'low carbon' economy were also released in July 2009. (The policy issues surrounding renewables and the 'low carbon economy' are inextricably linked.) The papers were:

- DECC, 'The UK Low Carbon Transition Plan', which outlined the path as to how the 34 per cent carbon emission cuts by 2020 (over 1990 levels, 18 per cent over 2008 levels) will be achieved.

- BIS and DECC, 'The UK Low Carbon Industrial Strategy (LCIS)', which set out a series of active government interventions to support industries critical to meeting the CO_2 emissions targets and 'tackling climate change'.

- DfT, 'Low Carbon Transport: a greener future'.

The Renewables Obligation (RO): The main features are:

- The RO is the obligation placed on licensed electricity suppliers to deliver a specified amount of their electricity from eligible renewable sources. It is designed to incentivise the generation of electricity from eligible renewable sources in the United Kingdom.

- It was introduced in England & Wales and in a different form (the Renewables Obligation (Scotland)) in Scotland in April 2002 and in Northern Ireland in April 2005. The RO places an obligation on licensed electricity suppliers in the United Kingdom to source an increasing proportion of electricity from renewable sources.

- This obligation level was initially set at three per cent for 2002-03 and had risen to 9.1 per cent of electricity supplied to customers in England & Wales and Scotland (3.0 per cent for Northern Ireland) in 2008-09 (source: OFGEM). The current target level is 9.7 per cent for 2009-10, rising to 15.4 per cent by 2015-16 for England & Wales (source: DECC).

- Eligible renewable generators receive Renewable Obligation Certificates (ROCs) for each MWh of electricity generated. These certificates can then be sold to electricity suppliers.

- In order to fulfil their obligation, suppliers can either present enough certificates to cover the required percentage of their output, or they can pay a 'buy-out' price for any shortfall.

- The cost of ROCs is effectively paid by all electricity consumers, since electricity suppliers pass this cost on as an increase in the tariff for the electricity they sell.

Reserves: Oil and gas reserves relate to the quantities identified as being present in underground cavities. The actual amounts that can be recovered, and considered economically worthwhile to recover, depend on the level of technology available and the price. These continually change—hence the level of the UK's reserves can change quite independently of whether or not new 'geological' reserves have been identified

Secondary fuels: These are fuels derived from natural sources of energy. For example, electricity generated from burning coal, gas or oil is a secondary fuel, as are coke and coke oven gas.

Thermal sources of electricity: These include coal, oil, natural gas, nuclear, landfill gas, sewage gas, municipal solid waste, farm waste, tyres, poultry litter, short rotation coppice, straw, coke oven gas, blast furnace gas, waste products from chemical processes.

Annex 2: Renewable Energy: tables

Table 4.1: EU Renewables Directive (2008), national overall targets for the chare of energy from renewable sources in final consumption of energy in 2020 (%)

	Share of energy from renewable sources in final consumption of energy, 2005 (%)	Target for share of energy from renewable sources in final consumption of energy, 2020 (%)	Arithmetic increase in share required (%)
UK	1.3	15	13.7
Spain	6.9	20	13.1
Denmark	17.0	30	13.0
Ireland	3.1	16	12.9
Germany	5.8	18	12.2
Italy	5.2	17	11.8
Netherlands	2.4	14	11.6
EU average	8.5	20	11.5
Belgium	2.25	13	10.8
Austria	23.3	34	10.7
Portugal	20.5	31	10.5
Cyprus	2.9	13	10.1
Luxembourg	0.9	11	10.1
Malta	0.0	10	10.0
France	10.3	20	9.7
Finland	28.5	38	9.5
Greece	8.7	18	9.3
Sweden	39.8	49	9.2
Slovenia	16.0	25	9.0
Hungary	4.3	13	8.7
Lithuania	15.0	23	8.0
Poland	7.2	15	7.8
Slovakia	6.7	14	7.3
Latvia	34.9	42	7.1
Estonia	18.0	25	7.0
Czech Republic	6.1	13	6.9
Bulgaria	9.4	16	6.6
Romania	17.8	24	6.2

Source: Commission of the European Communities, *Proposal for a Directive of the European Parliament and of the Council on the promotion of the use of energy from renewable sources*, January 2008, annex1, updated and EUIG.

Table 4.2: Renewable Energy Strategy: Impact Assessments, present value, £bn, 2008 prices, 2010-2030 (20 years), main estimates.

Policy Option	Description	Costs	Benefits	Net benefit
A	Share of renewables by sector: 29% large scale electricity; 12% heat; 10% transport; 2% small scale electricity	£60bn	£5bn	-£55bn
B	32% large scale electricity; 8.5% heat; 8% transport; 10% small scale electricity	£69bn	£4bn	-£66bn
C	24% large scale electricity; 12% heat; 12% transport; 3.5% small scale electricity, small STP (Severn Tidal Power) scheme	£57bn	£6bn	-£52bn
D	29% large scale electricity; 12% heat; 10% transport; 2% small scale electricity, trading	£57bn	£4bn	-£53bn

Sources: DECC, *Impact Assessment of UK Renewable Energy Strategy*, July 2009, www.decc.gov.uk. Data exclude ancillary costs/benefits of air quality factors; rounding errors in the table.

Annex 3: Energy Units

Joule: A generic unit of energy, equal to the energy dissipated by an electrical current of 1 ampere driven by 1 volt for 1 second.

Kilojoule (KJ) = 10^3 joules

Megajoule (MJ) = 10^6 joules

Gigajoule (GJ) = 10^9 joules

Terajoule (TJ) = 10^{12} joules

Megawatt and megawatt hour: A 1 MW (megawatt) power-generating unit running for 1 hour produces 1 megawatt hour (MWh) of electrical energy. MWe is used to emphasise when electricity is being measured and MWt is used when heat ('thermal') is being measured.

Therm: A common unit of measurement of energy.

Tonne of oil equivalent (toe): A common unit of measurement for energy. Million tonnes of oil equivalent (Mtoe) measure is frequently used.

Watt (W): A unit of electrical power, the conventional unit to measure a rate of flow of energy. One watt amounts to 1 joule per second.

Kilowatt (KW) = 10^3 watts

Megawatt (MW) = 10^6 watts

Gigawatt (GW) = 10^9 watts

Terawatt (TW) = 10^{12} watts

Watt hour (Wh): The watt hour is a measure of work, the watt is a measure of power. The amount of wattage times the amount of time is the amount of work done. It is not used in the International System of Units (SI). The SI unit of energy is the joule (J), equal to one watt second. The kilowatt hour is commonly used, though, especially for measuring electric energy. One watt hour is equivalent to 3,600 joules (there being 3,600 seconds in an hour).

Kilowatt hour (KWh) = 10^3 watt hours

Megawatt hour (MWh) = 10^6 watt hours

Gigawatt hour (GWh) = 10^9 watt hours

Terawatt hour (TWh) = 10^{12} watt hours

Note also the following conversions:

One tonne of oil equivalent	11,630 kilowatt hours (KWh)
One tonne of oil equivalent	41,868,000 kilojoules (KJ)
1 watt hour (Wh)	3,600 joules (J)
1 kilowatt hour (KWh)	3,600 kilojoules (KJ)
1 megawatt hour (MWh)	3,600 megajoules (MJ)
1 gigawatt hour (GWh)	3,600 gigajoules (GJ)
1 terawatt hour (TWh)	3,600 terajoules (TJ)

Notes

1: British Energy Policy

1   Principally China, the USA, Russia, India, Japan and Germany.

2   Available from DECC's website: www.decc.gov.uk

3   Collectively the EU's policies of (i) cutting carbon emissions by 20% by 2020, (ii) meeting 20% of energy consumption by renewables by 2020 and (iii) reducing primary energy use by 20% compared with projected levels by 2020 are known as the 20:20:20 targets.

4   HM Government, 'Building Britain's Future, Carbon Budgets' factsheet, available from www.decc.gov.uk, announced April 2009.

5   Dieter Helm, 'Don't blow our £100 billion on wind power', *The Times*, 17 July 2009.

6   The annexes provide more information about the Renewables Directive. Note that nuclear generated electricity is not regarded as a renewable source.

7   See Ruth Lea, 'Britain's renewable energy targets are quite unrealistic', Arbuthnot Banking Group, *Perspective*, 5 May 2008, for further discussion.

8   Further information is available in the annexes.

9   BERR, *UK Renewable Energy Strategy consultation document*, June 2008, available from www.berr.gov.uk, www.bis.gov.uk or www.decc.gov.uk.

10 The energy division of BERR and the climate change responsibilities of DEFRA were transferred to the new Department of Energy and Climate Change (DECC) in October 2008.

11 DECC, 'UK at forefront of a low carbon economic revolution', press release, 15 July 2009, available from www.decc.gov.uk.

12 The Impact Assessments of the UK *Renewable Energy Strategy* are shown in annex 2, table 2.

13 The individual papers are to be found on various government websites: www.bis.gov.uk, www.decc.gov.uk, www.dft.gov.uk and www.hmg.gov.uk/lowcarbon.

14 Note that BERR was subsumed in the new Department of Business, Innovation and Skills (BIS) in June 2009.

15 Pöyry, *Energy Consulting, Compliance costs for meeting the 20% renewable energy target in 2020: a report to the Department for Business, Enterprise and Regulatory Reform (BERR)*, March 2008.

16 Under Pöyry's least-cost scenario, the UK would meet its 15% compliance target for 2020 by 2 means: (i) by increasing renewables capacity (which would account for 10.4% of the 15%) and (ii) by buying permits (which would account for the remaining 4.6% of the 15%).

17 OFGEM, *Project Discovery*, February 2010.

2: The Impact of High Energy Costs on Energy Intensive Users

1   Ian Fells and Candida Whitmill, 'Finding the energy to keep UK manufacturing going', in Ruth Lea (ed.), *Nations Choose Prosperity*, Civitas, July 2009.

2   Roundtable discussion co-sponsored by Civitas and the ERA Foundation and held at the Royal Academy of Engineering on 18 November 2009.

3   Pöyry, *Energy Consulting, Compliance costs for meeting the 20% renewable energy target in 2020: a report to the Department for Business, Enterprise and Regulatory Reform (BERR)*, March 2008, available from www.berr.gov.uk

4   Carl Mortishead, 'Europe fails chemistry test as industry heads east', *The Times*, 7 October 2009, reported that there were possible threats to Shell's Stanlow refinery, Ineos's Grangemouth plant and Petrolplus in Teesside.

5   *Economist*, 'Europe and inscrutable China', 23 January 2010.

6   BBC News, '400 jobs to go at zinc works', 18 February 2003, available on www.bbc.co.uk/news.

7   EIUG press release, 'Industry demands action to secure gas supplies next winter', 15 May 2006, available on www.eiug.org.uk.

8   EIUG, 'Soaring energy prices cripple energy intensive manufacturing', July 2006.

9   BBC News, 'Metal plant will close next month', 13 August 2009.

10 *Daily Telegraph*, 'Neat double blow knocks out British aluminium industry', 16 August 2009.

11 Robin Pagnamenta, 'Digital Britain in jeopardy as power houses move abroad', *The Times*, 27 July 2009.

12 See Ruth Lea, 'Introduction: manufacturing industry in Britain', in *Nations Choose Prosperity*, Civitas, July 2009.

13 UK Trade and Investment, *Chemicals – the UK advantage: adding value for global investors and industry*, January 2009, on www.uktradeinvest.gov.uk

14 LECG Limited, Report to Ineos Chlor Limited, the evaluation of options for the chlor-alkali plant at Runcorn, main report, September 2001.